WHAT WOULD JESUS DO TO RISE ABOVE STRESS?

© 1998 by Daniel D. Grippo
Published by One Caring Place
Abbey Press
St. Meinrad, Indiana 47577

Library of Congress Catalog Number
97-78272

ISBN 0-87029-312-5

Book design by Aaron Presler

Printed in the United States of America

About the **WWJD** Books...

WWJD?—What Would Jesus Do? All of Christian belief and practice is summed up in this deceptively simple question. How can we live in love every day, as Jesus would? How can we respond with faith and hope to the problems of our lives?

As we struggle to cope with the crisis of the day—how can we do what Jesus would do?

The **WWJD Books From One Caring Place** show modern believers how to use these four little letters as a touchstone for coping with life's biggest challenges. Each lefthand page is a meditation on what Jesus would do to deal with the particular problem. Each righthand page presents a relevant Scripture passage—the Old Testament words that inspired Jesus' life, or what Jesus himself said, did, and taught in the New Testament. Drawing from the Word of God revealed in the Scriptures and in the life of Jesus, we find the strength and guidance to follow in his footsteps as we cope with our own life challenges.

Whether you read this book straight through from cover to cover, or randomly choose an inspiration for the day, may it lead you ever deeper into the Way, the Truth, and the Life of Christ. And may it remind you in the midst of every problem you face, at each juncture throughout your day: What Would Jesus Do?

Introduction

A little stress is a good thing: we all need some to "get the juices flowing." But when those juices reach the boiling point, we're in trouble. Too much stress is bad for our relationships and for our health—both physical and spiritual.

As a human being, Jesus knew stress. The Gospels recount many instances of his fear and fatigue, his anger and anguish. Yet at the same time, he knew that the best way to handle stress is through faith in a God who is always with us and who wants only the best for us.

Think of the story of Jesus asleep in the boat during the storm (Mark 4:37-40; Matthew 8:23-27; Luke 8:22-25).

The disciples are stressed out—to put it mildly—by the storm. When they wake Jesus, he asks them a simple question: "Why are you afraid?" and then provides the answer by way of another question: "Have you still no faith?"

Faith—in ourselves, in others, and in God—can go a long way toward beating stress. Sure, stressful situations are often beyond our control. But much stress comes from our responses to situations. Do we panic? Imagine the worst? Fly into a rage? Or can we learn to maintain—or at least recover—our calm by trusting God to help us through whatever it is we are facing?

Consider this book as a sort of "stress escape valve." When the pressure builds, allow yourself to rest in the calm of a Scripture verse and a brief meditation. Better yet, before the pressure builds, use this book to gain a sense of balance and perspective, to help you keep potentially stressful situations under control. Let these meditations help you touch the deep, calm, stress-free center where God resides and trust abounds. Go there often. God awaits you.

That's what Jesus would do!

JESUS WOULD...

Share the load

A certain amount of stress is natural and healthy. It's what keeps us going. The key is to figure out when stress is helping and when it's hurting, and to do something about it when it's hurting.

If you're feeling stressed, know that you're not alone. Everybody gets stressed at one time or another. So take a deep breath and relax. There are things you can do to help yourself, and you're in good company—even Jesus felt stress!

JESUS SAID...

Stress happens to all

"I have a baptism with which to be baptized, and what stress I am under until it is completed!"

LUKE 12:50

JESUS WOULD...

Take time apart

Feeling stressed? Find a time and place to quiet down. Until you allow yourself some quiet time, all you'll hear is the sound of your own static-producing stress.

Go to a private room, a wooded field, a quiet church—wherever you need to be in order to stop the world for a minute and get off. Don't worry—it'll still be there when you come back, but you'll be refreshed and centered!

JESUS DID...

Pray in a quiet place

In the morning, while it was still very dark, he got up and went out to a deserted place, and there he prayed.

MARK 1:35

Jesus Would...

Ask God for a hand

God is the most underutilized natural resource in the universe! God is waiting to help, but too often we don't bother asking.

Maybe you think you need to figure it out on your own. (You don't!) Or maybe you don't really believe God cares enough to help. (God does!) When the stress gets to be too much, turn to the One who is waiting to lend a hand.

JESUS READ...

Call upon the Lord

In my distress I called upon the Lord; to my God I cried for help. From his temple he heard my voice, and my cry to him reached his ears.

PSALM 18:6

JESUS WOULD...

Ask for what is needed

Stress often comes about when we don't have the right "tools"—physical, financial, emotional, and spiritual—for the challenge at hand. Once you figure out the things you need in order to get a job done or problem solved, you're well on your way.

Ask friends, family, loved ones, and caring professionals for help. Most importantly, ask God for what you need—you have Jesus' promise that you'll receive it!

JESUS SAID...

'The door will be opened'

"Ask and it will be given you; search, and you will find; knock, and the door will be opened for you."

LUKE 11:9

JESUS WOULD...

Sort out priorities

Sometimes we get so busy we lose touch with the things that matter most. When our deepest values conflict with our daily pursuits, stress results—big time.

Use the "fire drill" method to get at your priorities: in a big fire, who and what would you save first? Make a list. This puts things into perspective quickly!

Once you have a list, focus more time and attention on your top priorities, and cut back on some of the less important stuff. Watch your stress level take a nosedive!

JESUS SAID...

The heart holds the treasure

"For where your treasure is, there your heart will be also."

LUKE 12:34

JESUS WOULD...

Simplify

Once you've identified things that are getting in the way of your peace of mind, it's time to make some changes. Change involves some "uprooting" of the "weeds" that are choking you with stress.

For instance, maybe you spend too much time working and worrying about money, and not enough time relaxing and slowing down. Don't let the weeds of busyness choke off the life of your spirit. Clear away the clutter and make some time for your soul to catch up with you!

JESUS SAID...

Avoid the thorns

"Other seed fell among thorns, and the thorns grew up and choked it, and it yielded no grain."

MARK 4:7

JESUS WOULD...

Be content

"There's never enough..." starts many a stress-filled tale of woe. While it's certainly not good to go hungry, homeless, or without essential services, many of us are dissatisfied despite having everything we could possibly need. We simply want more.

The fact is, when we have faith that God will provide, we already have everything we need. So next time you've got a bad case of the "never-enough" blues, take a deep breath and thank God for all you do have—including that deep breath of air.

JESUS TAUGHT...

Have confidence in God

Keep your lives free from the love of money, and be content with what you have; for he has said, "I will never leave you or forsake you." So we can say with confidence, "The Lord is my helper; I will not be afraid. What can anyone do to me?"

HEBREWS 13:5-6

JESUS WOULD...

Focus on service, not power

So much stress is related to turf battles and power plays: "This is mine!" "Hey, I'm in charge here!" But by focusing on service, as Jesus did, instead of power, you align yourself with the natural forces of goodness.

Find ways to help out—in your family, community, school, church, or workplace. Surprise people by going the extra mile. Let someone else go ahead of you for a change, whether in a traffic jam or a lunch line. Watch your stress melt when you no longer need to be Number One all the time.

JESUS SAID...

The first must be last

He asked them, "What were you arguing about on the way?" But they were silent, for on the way they had argued with one another who was the greatest. He sat down, called the twelve, and said to them, "Whoever wants to be first must be last of all and servant of all."

MARK 9:33-35

JESUS WOULD...

Do one thing at a time

Multi-tasking is becoming a way of life. We juggle family obligations, work, social life, school, household chores, errands—and stress has a field day!

Next time you find yourself wolfing down a sandwich while listening to the radio, carrying on a conversation, making out your "To Do" list, and paging through a magazine—Hold everything! Just eat that sandwich...slowly.

There, isn't that better? Apply the same lesson to other areas of your life.

JESUS SAID...

Choose the better part

Mary...sat at the Lord's feet and listened to what he was saying. But Martha was distracted by her many tasks; so she came to him and asked, "Lord, do you not care that my sister has left me to do all the work by myself? Tell her then to help me." But the Lord answered her, "Martha, Martha, you are worried and distracted by many things; there is need of only one thing. Mary has chosen the better part."

LUKE 10:39-42

JESUS WOULD...

Approach life with childlike wonder

When we lose the ability to relax and laugh, to be surprised and delighted by life, it's a pretty sure bet that stress is doing some serious damage. Watch a child at play—completely absorbed, oblivious to time, in touch with the present moment and the wonder of creation.

Make time for the child within you to play, to laugh, to walk barefoot in the tall grass. After all, childhood is too much fun to be enjoyed only by the very young!

JESUS SAID...

Enter the kingdom as a child

"Truly I tell you, whoever does not receive the kingdom of God as a little child will never enter it."

MARK 10:15

JESUS WOULD...

Turn it over to God

Think of the times you've stayed up half the night worrying about something over which you had little control, only to discover the next day—bleary-eyed and all—that things worked out anyway.

If a problem is causing you great stress, make a conscious decision to lift the burden off your shoulders and hand it to God. Don't worry about God dropping it, either. God is used to such burdens—after all, there's a whole universe to look after!

JESUS READ...

God will uphold you

Cast your burden on the Lord, and he will sustain you.

PSALM 55:22

JESUS WOULD...

Trust that God will provide

Have you ever turned a problem over to God, only to take it right back? Maybe you didn't really believe God could help. Maybe you got tired of waiting for a response (God's answers don't always come on our schedule). Whatever the reason, the end result is the same—more stress, right back on your shoulders!

Next time you turn over a problem, really turn it over. Trust God to take care of it. You'll be glad you did.

JESUS READ...

God answers your call

Answer me when I call, O God of my right! You gave me room when I was in distress....The Lord hears when I call to him.

PSALM 4:1, 3

JESUS WOULD...

Ask for support

Do you feel like you alone are carrying the problems of the world on your shoulders?

Here's the good news—whatever the challenge, whatever the problem, you don't have to go it alone. Invite others into your life, and watch the storm clouds disappear.

If you don't know where to turn, pick up the Yellow Pages and look under "Support Groups" or "Hotlines." Reach out, as Jesus did—others will be there to take your hand!

JESUS SAID...

Find a friend in need

Jesus went with them to a place called Gethsemane; and he said to his disciples, "Sit here while I go over there and pray." He...began to be grieved and agitated. Then he said to them, "I am deeply grieved, even to death; remain here, and stay awake with me."

MATTHEW 26:36-38

JESUS WOULD...

Be a bearer of good news

It's easy to focus on the negative—there's certainly plenty of it around! But why add to your stress by reinforcing it with a gloomy outlook?

Make a quick list of five things you're grateful for—simple things, the kind of stuff we take for granted every day. Once your mood has brightened, share some good cheer with others, and watch the magic begin!

JESUS READ...

Be of good cheer

Anxiety weighs down the human heart, but a good word cheers it up.

PROVERBS 12:25

JESUS WOULD...

Treat others well

A certain amount of conflict is unavoidable in human relationships, but we can minimize the damage by maximizing our generosity. When we go out of our way to be kind to others, we go a long way toward easing the many stresses of daily living.

No small act of kindness is wasted. Next time you're backed up in traffic, ease up and let someone in ahead of you. As the bumper sticker says: "Practice random acts of kindness."

JESUS SAID...

Do unto others

"Give to everyone who begs from you; and if anyone takes away your goods, do not ask for them again. Do to others as you would have them do to you."

LUKE 6:30-31

JESUS WOULD...

Indulge in an occasional treat

When was the last time you treated yourself to an ice-cream cone on a summer's eve, or took a luxurious hot bath on a cold, gray afternoon?

All of us need to be pampered now and then. The good things of the earth were made to be enjoyed—God delights in our delight. Stress melts away when we find healthy ways to enjoy life's many simple pleasures.

Treat yourself to something special today. You deserve it!

JESUS DID...

Let good times flow

As he sat at the table, a woman came with an alabaster jar of very costly ointment of nard, and she broke open the jar and poured the ointment on his head.

MARK 14:3

JESUS WOULD...

Listen to the music

Next time your stress level becomes unmanageable, try taking a musical interlude—ten minutes of soothing music. Make a tape of gentle music and keep it handy.

Quiet background music eases stress. It can help you get through the day with a bit more lift, and through the night with a bit more serenity.

Tune in!

JESUS READ...

Music soothes the soul

David took the lyre and played it with his hand, and Saul would be relieved and feel better, and the evil spirit would depart from him.

1 SAMUEL 16:23

JESUS WOULD...

Find peace within

We are sometimes our own worst enemy. We're quick to forgive others but slow to forgive ourselves. Yet being human means we're going to make mistakes.

Next time you mess up, step back for a minute and ask, "If my best friend did this, would I hold it against her?" Chances are, you'd forgive and forget. So how about treating yourself like a friend this time?

JESUS SAID...

Ease your troubled heart

"Peace I leave with you; my peace I give to you. I do not give to you as the world gives. Do not let your hearts be troubled, and do not let them be afraid."

JOHN 14:27

JESUS WOULD...

Live in peace with others

Peace begins at home. Find ways to make your corner of the world just a little less stressed, a little more tranquil: lower the volume, greet a neighbor, pitch in on a community anti-violence project.

Peace radiates outward like the warming rays of the sun. Be a bright light on the horizon, and watch stress melt into a peaceful, flowing river.

JESUS SAID...

Divided we fall

"Every kingdom divided against itself is laid waste, and no city or house divided against itself will stand."

MATTHEW 12:25

JESUS WOULD...

Build self-esteem

When we don't believe we deserve anything good in life, stress has a field day. Low self-esteem leads us to punish ourselves, which in turn leads to stress. "Put away your whips and chains," a wise counselor used to tell a client who was always blaming himself for everything.

Next time you find yourself beating yourself up, take a moment to think about what it means to be loved—really loved, deep-down loved—by the God of all creation. Now, isn't that better than punishing yourself all the time?

JESUS SAID...

God cherishes you

"Are not five sparrows sold for two pennies? Yet not one of them is forgotten in God's sight....Do not be afraid; you are of more value than many sparrows."

LUKE 12:6, 7

JESUS WOULD...

Encourage honesty

"Last year I was conceited; this year I'm perfect," goes the old joke. But deep down, don't we all tend to deny—or at least hide—our shortcomings? When we accept our own humanity and life's imperfections, we can avoid much anxiety.

Certain indigenous tribes are said to leave a small hole in each basket they weave; they believe that only God can create something perfect and complete.

Enjoy being an imperfect "basket." That way, you'll avoid being a basket case!

JESUS SAID...

The truth will set you free

Jesus said to her, "Go, call your husband, and come back." The woman answered him, "I have no husband." Jesus said to her, "You are right in saying, 'I have no husband'; for you have had five husbands, and the one you have now is not your husband. What you have said is true!"

JOHN 4:16-18

JESUS WOULD...

Value self-knowledge

To make mistakes is human; to learn from them is divine! When we look back on past stressful times, we realize that some of our choices have been less than wise.

No need to beat yourself up for past mistakes. Instead, think about how you can learn and grow from what you've experienced. Be thankful for the chance to get to know yourself better. You're on God's royal road to wisdom.

JESUS READ...

Let insight guide you

Get wisdom; get insight: do not forget, nor turn away from the words of my mouth. Do not forsake her, and she will keep you; love her, and she will guard you.

PROVERBS 4:5-6

JESUS WOULD...

Seek wisdom

There's a reason slow-motion sports replays are popular on television; slow motion allows us to see every move, to evaluate the wisdom of every position.

We can save ourselves a heap of trouble by slowing down long enough to think before we act. Try living today in slow motion. You may be amazed at how well—and wisely—you play the game!

JESUS READ...

'Your sleep will be sweet'

Keep sound wisdom and prudence, and they will be life for your soul and adornment for your neck. Then you will walk on your way securely and your foot will not stumble....When you lie down, your sleep will be sweet. Do not be afraid of sudden panic...for the Lord will be your confidence.

PROVERBS 3:21-23, 24, 25, 26

49

JESUS WOULD...

Live in the present

Much stress is anticipatory: we dread an imagined future that often fails to materialize. Meanwhile, we've lost our chance to live the present moment in peace.

As much as possible, try to remain in the present moment. When you do, you'll usually find you have the resources at hand to resolve whatever problem you face.

Stressed about tomorrow? Let tomorrow take care of itself. Seize the day!

JESUS SAID...

Don't borrow sorrow from tomorrow

"So do not worry about tomorrow, for tomorrow will bring worries of its own. Today's trouble is enough for today."

MATTHEW 6:34

JESUS WOULD...

Leave no room for anxiety

Anxiety usually involves stressful doubts about our ability to handle what's ahead: a work deadline, a relationship crisis, the results of a medical exam, or the approaching death of a loved one.

Life's uncertainties are hard to handle, but anxiety rarely helps—because it's focused on anticipated rather than real challenges. If you meet a bear in a forest, a high-anxiety adrenaline rush is entirely appropriate. But don't let imaginary bears haunt your mind and steal your serenity.

JESUS READ...

Be at peace

Banish anxiety from your mind.

ECCLESIASTES 11:10

JESUS WOULD...

Have confidence in God

Fear brings its own special brand of stress. If you lose a job, for example, the fear of running out of money can be so stressful that it keeps you from concentrating on finding another job.

Prayer, silent or spoken, allows us to bring our fears before God. For a bad case of fearful stress, the best remedy is to say two prayers and call on God in the morning!

JESUS READ...

Be not afraid

Do not fear, for I am with you, do not be afraid, for I am your God; I will strengthen you, I will help you, I will uphold you.

ISAIAH 41:10

JESUS WOULD...

Keep calm amid the turbulence

Sometimes the ride can get pretty bumpy for a while. Things may get a little crazy around the house, at the office, at school.

Next time things get out of hand, find your own still point in the turning world. Have faith that the situation will calm down. If you're having trouble staying calm, think of Jesus resting in the storm-tossed boat. Ask him to help you do the same.

JESUS DID...

Go with the flow

A great windstorm arose, and the waves beat into the boat, so that the boat was already being swamped. But he was in the stern, asleep on the cushion.

MARK 4:37-38

JESUS WOULD...

Trust that the storm will pass

Stormy weather—in the natural world and in our lives—can bring great stress. But even the worst of storms does pass.

At a time like this, it's best to seek shelter—physical, emotional, spiritual, whatever the case may call for—and ride out the storm. Call on God's protection.

At the same time, recall the quiet that has followed previous storms. Hold fast to the promise of calm contained in this new storm.

JESUS DID...

Calm down

They went to him and woke him up, shouting, "Master, Master, we are perishing!" And he woke up and rebuked the wind and the raging waves; they ceased, and there was a calm.

LUKE 8:24

JESUS WOULD...

Turn to prayer

Prayer is our first and best line of defense against stress. Prayer helps us find the still point at the center of our being. Research has shown prayer's calming power.

Another great thing about prayer is its flexibility: you can pray at home, in church, outdoors in nature, in a car or bus, in line at the supermarket.

So next time stress has you overwhelmed, take a five-minute "prayer break"—no matter where you are.

JESUS READ...

Prayer will lift you up

Therefore let all who are faithful offer prayer to you; at a time of distress, the rush of mighty waters shall not reach them.

PSALM 32:6

JESUS WOULD...

Trust in the power of prayer

Stress comes from second-guessing ourselves—and from second-guessing God. Jesus taught that prayer is only as effective as the trust of the person praying.

If we do our part—trusting that God indeed answers prayers—God will do the rest. God is standing by to help—in fact, to move mountains if necessary!

JESUS SAID...

It will be done for you

"Truly I tell you, if you say to this mountain, 'Be taken up and thrown into the sea,' and if you do not doubt in your heart, but believe that what you say will come to pass, it will be done for you. So I tell you, whatever you ask for in prayer, believe that you have received it, and it will be yours."

MARK 11:22-24

JESUS WOULD...

Find a quiet place for renewal

Stress is to the spirit as rust is to a car battery.

From time to time, our spiritual batteries need recharging. "Every three months or 3,000 miles" is a good rule of thumb for our spirits as well as our autos.

Plan to get away at least once every three months—once every season of the year. Go to a quiet place, a place that is holy for you, and "lie down in green pastures" for awhile. After your tune-up, listen to your spirit purr!

JESUS READ...

You will be restored

The Lord is my shepherd, I shall not want. He makes me lie down in green pastures; he leads me beside still waters; he restores my soul.

PSALM 23:1-3

JESUS WOULD...

Turn to the God within for refuge

Sometimes stress feels like a giant net entrapping us. The more we struggle, the more tangled we become.

When everything around you is chaotic, turn inward. Close your eyes. Listen to your own heartbeat as a way of quieting down. Picture God as a large, solid rock. Now touch the rock. Feel its solid, cool strength.

When we turn inward to find God, we find a fortress of strength that will not fail us.

JESUS READ...

Stand upon the rock

In you, O Lord, I seek refuge....Be a rock of refuge for me, a strong fortress to save me. You are indeed my rock and my fortress; for your name's sake lead me and guide me, take me out of the net that is hidden for me, for you are my refuge.

PSALM 31:1, 3-4

JESUS WOULD...

Recall God's love

Nothing beats stress like a little TLC, especially from God!

What is it that puts you in touch with God's love? A walk in the park? A nap in the sun? A visit with a child?

Whatever the source, go to it when stress has you feeling overwhelmed. Bask in God's love until the siege of stress is lifted.

JESUS READ...

The siege shall be lifted

Blessed be the Lord, for he has wondrously shown his stead-fast love to me when I was beset as a city under siege.

PSALM 31:21

JESUS WOULD...

Hold fast to God's love

Hardship has a way of coming between us and that which we need to feel most strongly at a time of great stress—God's love.

Don't let anything stand between you and that love. Realize that even when you're not feeling the love, it's still there, just as the sun is still shining on a dark, cloudy day.

God's love always burns brightly. Don't let the clouds of stress keep you from basking in it!

JESUS TAUGHT...

Nothing can keep us from God's love

Who will separate us from the love of Christ? Will hardship, or distress, or persecution, or famine, or nakedness, or peril, or sword?...For I am convinced that neither death nor life, nor angels, nor rulers, nor things present, nor things to come, nor powers, nor height, nor depth, nor anything else in all creation, will be able to separate us from the love of God in Christ Jesus our Lord.

ROMANS 8:35, 38-39

JESUS WOULD...

Listen for God's guidance

Listening is a great art, but we can't listen very well when there's a lot of noise—and nothing's as noisy as stress. How can God give us guidance when there's so much static in the air?

Try to turn down the volume long enough to let God's word in. (Having trouble figuring out what God wants you to do? The word *obey* actually comes from a word meaning "to listen.") To benefit from God's guidance, we need to learn to listen well.

JESUS READ...

Be at ease

Those who listen to me will be secure and will live at ease, without dread of disaster.

PROVERBS 1:33

JESUS WOULD...

Hear God in the silence

Silence can be kind of spooky, because we're accustomed to hearing so much noise. But silence allows us to hear the voice of God.

Silence also lets us listen to ourselves—to get in touch with our feelings and figure out what they are trying to tell us.

Next time stress has you wanting to scream, put a finger to your lips, take a deep breath, and say, "Shhhh." That's better. Now listen to the silence. It has a lot to say.

JESUS READ...

Silence speaks

He said, "Go out and stand on the mountain before the Lord, for the Lord is about to pass by." Now there was a great wind,…but the Lord was not in the wind; and after the wind an earthquake, but the Lord was not in the earthquake; and after the earthquake a fire, but the Lord was not in the fire; and after the fire a sound of sheer silence. When Elijah heard it, he wrapped his face in his mantle and went out and stood at the entrance of the cave. Then there came a voice to him.

1 KINGS 19:11-13

JESUS WOULD...

Leave it in God's hands

Ever play the game "Trust me"? You stand on a chair, close your eyes, and fall—an exhilarating moment of abandon—then the sure hands of your friends catch you.

Trust brings freedom. It's hard to pull off, but try to trust God with that overdue bill, tomorrow's job interview, the results of the CAT scan.

Tough? Sure. But imagine how much trust it took for the disciples to drop everything and follow Jesus.

Close your eyes and fall—into God's arms.

JESUS SAID...

Come, follow me

As Jesus was walking along, he saw a man called Matthew sitting at the tax booth; and he said to him, "Follow me." And he got up and followed him.

MATTHEW 9:9

JESUS WOULD...

Focus on the prize

Maybe you've heard the saying: "There goes someone who knows the price of everything and the value of nothing." Stress takes over when we lose sight of the things that matter most.

Spend a little time thinking about your values. For perspective, ask yourself what description of your life you'd want inscribed on your gravestone.

When we focus on our deepest beliefs and values, the more trivial stuff of daily life can't absorb all our attention or stress us out as much.

JESUS SAID...

'Consider the lilies'

"Consider the lilies of the field, how they grow; they neither toil nor spin, yet I tell you, even Solomon in all his glory was not clothed like one of these....Therefore do not worry....but strive first for the kingdom of God and his righteousness, and all these things will be given to you as well."

MATTHEW 6:28-29, 31, 33

JESUS WOULD...

Rest in love

When it comes to stress, here's the bottom line—whatever the problem, whatever the challenge, you don't have to go it alone.

Ask for help from those around you, and watch your burden lighten. Offer help to those around you, and watch your spirit lift.

Always keep in mind that Jesus is standing right at your side, ready to lighten your burden.

Lighten up!

JESUS SAID...

'My burden is light'

"Come to me, all you that are weary and are carrying heavy burdens, and I will give you rest. Take my yoke upon you, and learn from me; for I am gentle and humble in heart, and you will find rest for your souls. For my yoke is easy, and my burden is light."

MATTHEW 11:28

JESUS WOULD...

Say, 'Don't worry...Be happy!'

God wants our complete and total well-being. But too much stress can erode our health and happiness. Do everything you can to keep stress manageable, beginning with a decision not to let things "get to you" so often.

The more you choose a low-stress diet, the more God will be able to fill your plate with good things.

May the Peace of Christ be with you!

JESUS TAUGHT...

Rejoice!

Rejoice in the Lord always; again I will say, Rejoice. Let your gentleness be known to everyone. The Lord is near. Do not worry about anything, but in everything by prayer and supplication with thanksgiving let your requests be made known to God. And the peace of God, which surpasses all understanding, will guard your hearts and your minds in Christ Jesus.

PHILIPPIANS 4:4-7

WWJD Books
from One Caring Place

What Would Jesus Do...to Rise Above Stress?
What Would Jesus Do...to Live Anew After Loss?
What Would Jesus Do...to Live in Love Each Day?
What Would Jesus Do...to Find Meaning in Suffering?

Available at your favorite gift shop, bookstore,
or directly from:

One Caring Place
Abbey Press Publications
St. Meinrad, IN 47577
1-800-325-2511